Animal Worlds

Animals that work

Sue Barraclough

www.heinemann.co.uk/library
Visit our website to find out more information about **Heinemann Library** books.

To order:
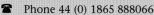
☎ Phone 44 (0) 1865 888066
▤ Send a fax to 44 (0) 1865 314091
▥ Visit the Heinemann Bookshop at www.heinemann.co.uk/library to browse our
catalogue and order online.

First published in Great Britain by
Heinemann Library, Halley Court, Jordan Hill,
Oxford OX2 8EJ, part of Harcourt Education.
Heinemann is a registered trademark of Harcourt
Education Ltd.

Editorial: Sarah Shannon and Dave Harris
Design: Jo Hinton-Malivoire and bigtop design ltd
Picture Research: Ruth Blair and Kay Altwegg
Production: Chloe Bloom

Originated by Modern Age
Printed and bound in China by South China
Printing Company

ISBN 0 431 00365 3 (hardback)
10 09 08 07 06
10 9 8 7 6 5 4 3 2 1

ISBN 0 431 00370 X (paperback)
10 09 08 07 06
10 9 8 7 6 5 4 3 2 1

British Library Cataloguing in Publication Data
Barraclough, Sue
    Animals that work. - (Animal worlds)
    636'.0886
A full catalogue record for this book is available
from the British Library.

Acknowledgements
The publishers would like to thank the following
for permission to reproduce photographs:
Alamy/Charlie Barland p. 19; Alamy/Paul Wayne
Wilson p. 11; Alamy/Shout p. 15; Ardea London
Ltd/John Daniels p. 8; Corbis/Dave Bartruff p. 20;
Corbis/Jim Craigmyle p. 12; Corbis/Kevin R.
Morris p. 6; Corbis/Paul A. Souders p. 10;
Corbis/Ron Sanford p. 18; Corbis/Tim Graham p.
22; Getty Images/Photodisc p. 13; Harcourt Index
p. 9; Jean Paul Ferrero/Ardea London Ltd p. 18;
Naturepl.com/Aflo p. 23; NHPA/Brian & Cherry
Alexander pp. 4, 5; NHPA/Danie Heuclin p. 15;
NHPA/E Hanumantha Rao p. 7; NHPA/Martin
Harvey p. 14; NHPA/Norburt Wu p. 21;
NHPA/Steve Robinson p. 17; Rex Features p. 16.

Cover photograph reproduced with permission
of photolibrary.com.

Every effort has been made to contact copyright
holders of any material reproduced in this book.
Any omissions will be rectified in subsequent
printings if notice is given to the publishers.

The paper used to print this book comes from
sustainable resources.

Contents

Animals that work

Some animals help us do things. They are called working animals.

These dogs pull sleds across the snow.

Different working animals

All kinds of animals can work.

Dogs run fast.
They can help
round up cattle.

Why do you think
this farmer rides the horse?

Strong animals help carry heavy loads.

This elephant uses its trunk to pick up logs.

Stables and kennels

Working animals need somewhere to sleep that is warm and dry.

Horses live in stables.

Dogs live in kennels.

Food and water

All animals need to eat food to give them energy.

Horses like to eat hay.

Animals at work

Animals help people in many ways.

Donkeys can help carry heavy loads.

Guide dogs help their owners by leading them around safely.

Learning how

Working animals have to learn how to do their jobs.

These elephants learn how to move huge logs.

14

This dog learns how to find people who are lost in the snow.

Special jobs

Some animals have special jobs.

Police horses are big and strong. They carry police officers on patrol.

Dogs have a good sense of smell. They use their noses to find things.

Sniff! Sniff!

17

Making noises

Working animals make all kinds of noises.

woof!

Guard dogs bark loudly.

18

Holidays

Working animals need time to relax and play.

These army horses
are having a day
out at the beach.

Caring and cleaning

Working animals need special care.

They need plenty of exercise, and to be brushed and cleaned.

All animals need a place
to rest and sleep.

Index

Notes for adults

This series supports a young child's knowledge and understanding of their world. The following Early Learning Goals are relevant to the series:

• Find out about and identify some features of living things, objects, and events that they observe.

• Develop communication, language and literacy by imitating different animal sounds, and to notice and describe similarities and differences.

These books will help children extend their vocabulary, as they will hear some new words. Since words are used in context in the book this should enable young children to gradually incorporate them into their own vocabulary.

This series investigates a variety of animals by looking at distinguishing features and characteristics and by exploring their different environments.

Follow-up activities:

Encourage children to draw and record what they have learned about working animals, and to notice any differences or similarities when compared to other animals in the series.